WIDE YOUR MOUTH!

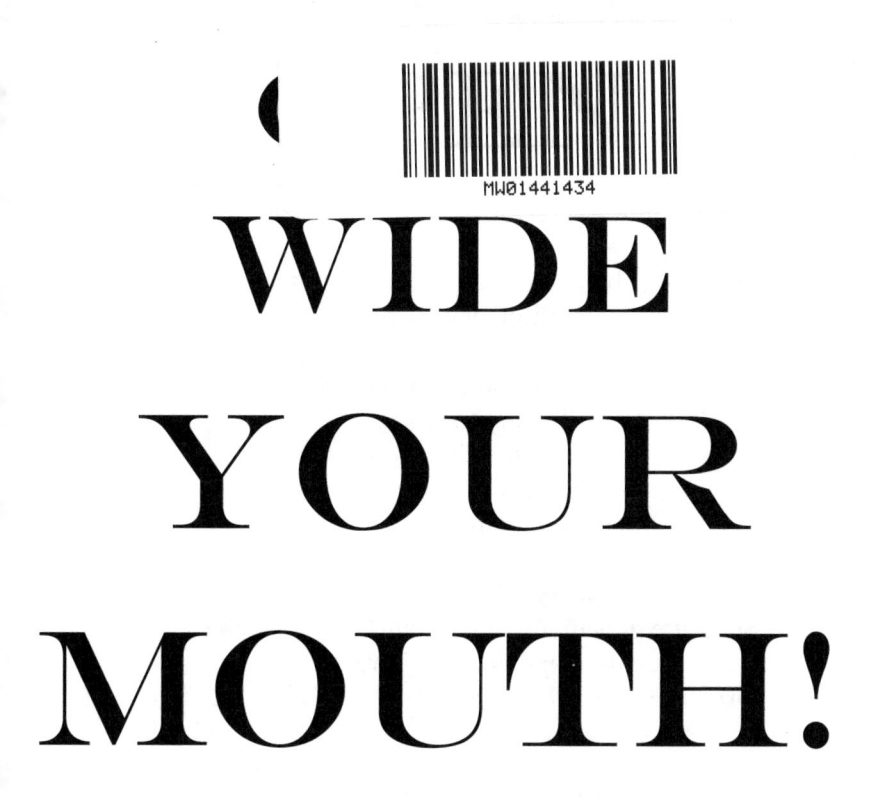

A 31 Day Daily Devotional

TAMMY M. ISAAC, MDiv

Open Wide Your Mouth!
Copyright © 2021 by Tammy M. Isaac

Copies of this book are available at quantity discounts
for bulk purchases.

For more information, contact:
Tammy M. Isaac
www.tamsisaac.org
www.close-the-door.org
Email: tammymisaac@aol.com

Unless otherwise noted,
Scripture quotations taken from The Holy Bible,
New International Version® NIV®
Copyright © 1973 1978 1984 2011 by Biblica, Inc. TM
Used by permission. All rights reserved worldwide.

ISBN: 978-0-578-82740-7

Printed in the United States of America.
All rights reserved. No part of this book may be reproduced or transmitted in any form or by any means, electronic or mechanical, including photocopying, recording, or any information storage and retrieval system, without written permission of the publisher except for brief quotations used in reviews, written specifically for inclusion in newspapers, blogs, or magazines.

Cover Design:
Candice Kilgore, Think. Create. Build.
www.thinkcreatebuild.com

Book Production:
Marvin D. Cloud, mybestseller Publishing Company
marvin@marvindcloud.com

*I am the LORD your God, who brought you up out of Egypt.
Open wide your mouth and I will fill it. —Psalm 81:10*

DEDICATION

This book is dedicated to my dear friend, Likeythia Blackmon who in this season has learned to open her mouth toward God. She is the inspiration for this devotional as I am watching her journey through a difficult season in her in life. I love you and I count it a blessing to be your friend.

ACKNOWLEDGMENTS

I give God all the glory and honor to be able to produce this written work in a time of a pandemic. I am grateful that He spoke to me and guided me in completing this work. I also want to thank everyone who supports my writing and suggest I should continue to write more.

TABLE OF CONTENTS

Introduction	1
Day 1-10	23
Open Wide Your Mouth	35
Day 11-20	45
A Closed Mouth Don't Get Fed	59
Day 21-31	63
Bibliography	75
About the Author	79

The Hebrew term for mouth is
פ *(pey).*

Sing for joy to God our strength;
shout aloud to the God of Jacob!
Begin the music, strike the timbrel,
play the melodious harp and lyre.
Sound the ram's horn at the New Moon,
and when the moon is full, on the day
of our festival;
this is a decree for Israel,
an ordinance of the God of Jacob.
When God went out against Egypt,
he established it as a statute for Joseph.
I heard an unknown voice say:
"I removed the burden from their shoulders;
their hands were set free from the basket.
In your distress you called, and I rescued you,
I answered you out of a thundercloud;
I tested you at the waters of Meribah.
Hear me, my people, and I will warn you—
if you would only listen to me, Israel!
You shall have no foreign god among you;
you shall not worship any god other than me.
I am the Lord your God,
who brought you up out of Egypt.
Open wide your mouth and I will fill it.
"But my people would not listen to me;
Israel would not submit to me.
So I gave them over to their stubborn hearts
to follow their own devices.

*"If my people would only listen to me,
if Israel would only follow my ways,
how quickly I would subdue their enemies
and turn my hand against their foes!
Those who hate the Lord would cringe before
him, and their punishment would last forever.
But you would be fed with the finest of wheat;
with honey from the rock I would satisfy you.
Psalm 81:1-16 (NIV)*

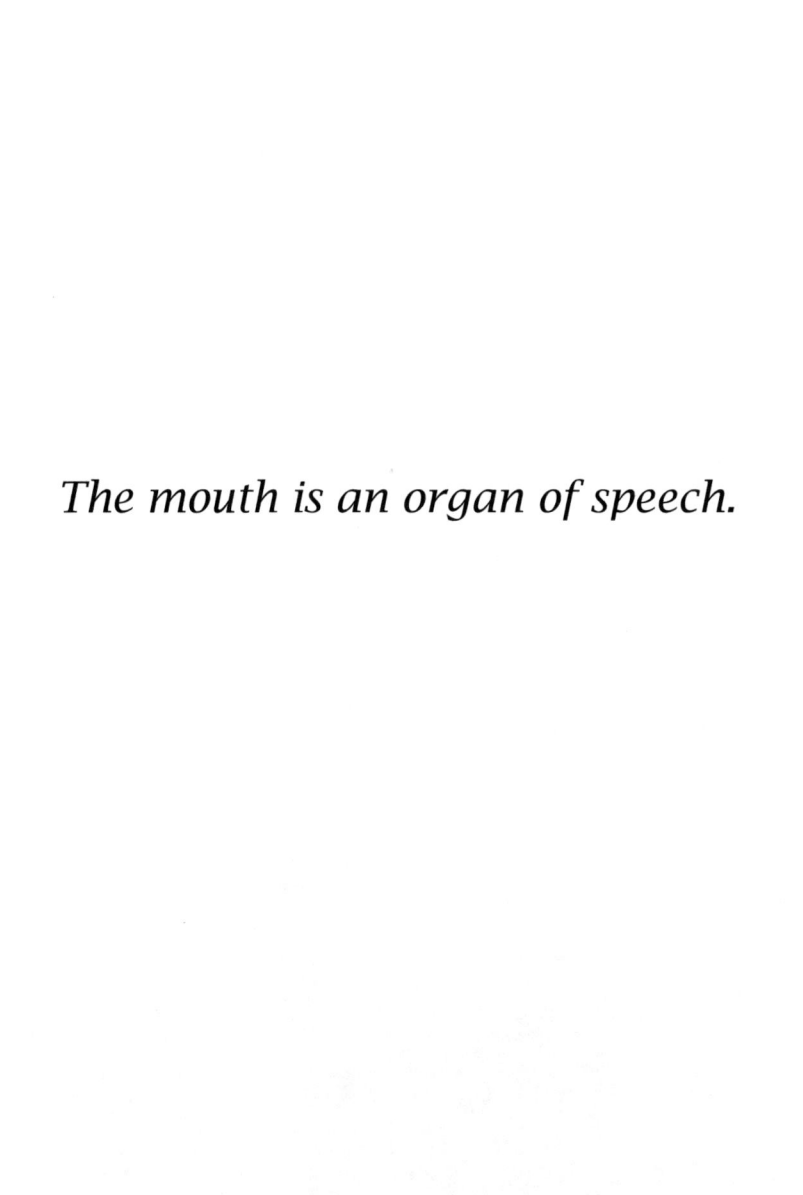

The mouth is an organ of speech.

INTRODUCTION

The year 2020 on the Gregorian calendar coincides with The Hebrew year 5780. "The Hebrew alphabet, the holy language of the Bible… consists of 22 letters, all consonants, none of which are lowercase. Each letter has its own sound and numerical value… The letters and the words they form are holy, with layers of meaning from the literal to the mystical.[1] The Hebrew letter for the number 80 in the year 5780 is "פ(Pey)"[2]. Pey, is the symbol of the mouth. The year 5780 ushered us into the start of a new year (2020) and a new decade, the decade of the mouth.

The main channel through which breath is exchanged is through the mouth. "The mouth is the expression of the breath. Through our mouths the breath becomes vocalized."[3]

---

[1] "The Hebrew Alphabet," Chabad, last modified 2020, https:// www.chabad.org/library/article_cdo/aid/4069287/jewish/The-Hebrew-Alphabet.htm.

[2] "H6310-peh-Strong's Hebrew Lexicon (KJV)." Blue Letter Bible. Accessed 28 Nov, 2020. https://www.blueletterbible.org//lang/lexicon/lexicon.cfm?Strongs=H6310&t=KJV

[3] Rena Perozich, "The Year to Say What You've Seen That You Want!," The Remarkable Blog, November 8, 2019, http://rpmdaily.net/blog/the-year-to-say-what-youve-seen-that-you-want#:~:text=%E2%80%9CPey%E2%80%9D%20is%20the%20Hebrew%20letter,picture%20symbol%20of%20a%20mouth.&text=Through%20our%20mouths%20the%20breath,Breath%20of%20the%20Ho.

The mouth is an organ of speech. It is an external "opening or orifice (a well, river, cave, etc.)"[4]. The mouth is an entry and exit way, it is an organ for eating and drinking.

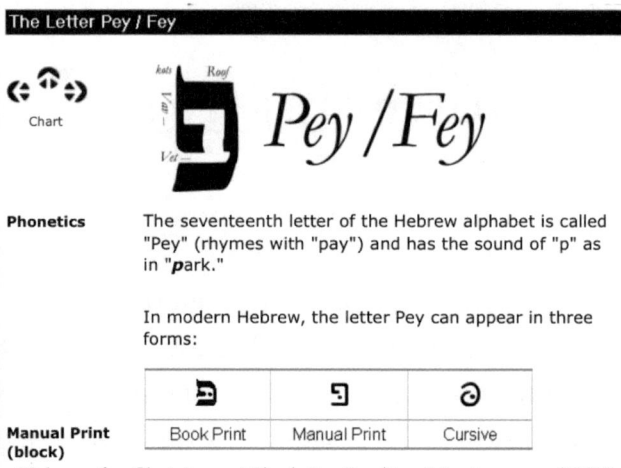

The Letter Pey / Fey			
Chart	פ Pey /Fey		
Phonetics	The seventeenth letter of the Hebrew alphabet is called "Pey" (rhymes with "pay") and has the sound of "p" as in "**p**ark."		
	In modern Hebrew, the letter Pey can appear in three forms:		
Manual Print (block)	Book Print	Manual Print	Cursive

Hebrew for Christians. "The letter Pey/Fey." Last accessed 2020. https:// hebrew4Christians.com/Grammar/Unit_One/Aleph-Bet/Pey/pey.html

In an article titled "Of Birds Lips and Baby Hawks" by Alisa Kline, she shares that "when hungry baby birds open their mouths as wide as they can this exposes a colorful inner mouth. The opening of the mouth is called a gape. A gape is a wide opening of the mouth as the result of hunger. The Gape is a signal that there is a need. The configuration of colors and shapes of the baby birds' inner mouth is a signal to the mother bird to put food into the baby's mouth."[5] Charles Surgeon

---

[4]"H6310 - peh - Strong's Hebrew Lexicon (KJV)." Blue Letter Bible. Accessed 28 Nov, 2020. https://www.blueletterbible.org//lang/lexicon/lexicon.cfm?Strongs=H6310&t=KJV

[5]Alisa Kline, "Of Birds Lips and Baby Hawks," Buffalo Bayou (blog), n.d., https://buffalobayou.org/blog/of-bird-lips-and-baby-hawks/#:~:text=There%20 are%20many%20studies%20showing,in%20the%20ultra%2Dviolet%20 spectrum.&text=That%20is%20why%20as%20a,less%20likely%20to%20be% 20eaten.

Introduction

says, "What makes a young bird open their mouth wide except for hunger? They do so because they need food." But not only do they open wide their mouths, but they do so toward their mother whom they know can and will feed them with what they need to grow healthy and strong. "Studies have shown that mother birds can recognize their own offspring by the gape coloring… and suggest that baby birds advertise their fitness through their gape coloring and [the mother bird] use this information to give extra food to their healthiest baby birds."[6] If the baby birds do not open wide their mouths, then they will not be feed. Closed mouths don't get fed! Open wide your mouth!

Inside the letter Pey is found another letter. "The inner space of the letter Pey reveals the letter Bet."[7] The letter Bet is a symbol of a "house or dwelling place."[8] Home is a dwelling place, where one spends most of their time. The phrase "Home is where the heart is", is a popular phrase that has been heard or used a time or two throughout the years. In his book, Collected Poems, Prose, and Plays, Robert Frost, says, "Home is the place that, when you have to go there, they have to take you in." Dorothy, played by Judy Garland, in the film The Wizard of Oz said, "There's no place like home" after experiencing being in a place of unfamiliarity, uncertainty, and unacceptance.

---

[6] Alisa Kline, "Of Birds Lips and Baby Hawks," Buffalo Bayou (blog), n.d., https://buffalobayou.org/blog/of-bird-lips-and-baby-hawks/#:~:text=There%20 are%20many%20studies%20showing,in%20the%20ultra%2Dviolet%20spectrum. &text=That%20is%20why%20as%20a,less%20likely%20to%20be% 20eaten.

[7] "The Letter Pey/fey," Hebrew for Christians, last modified 2020, https://www.hebrew4christians.com/Grammar/Unit_One/Aleph-Bet/Pey/pey.html.

[8] "The Letter Bet/vet," Hebrew for Christians, last modified 2020, https://www.hebrew4christians.com/Grammar/Unit_One/Aleph-Bet/Bet/bet.html.

When you are not welcomed or accepted in certain places and among certain people, home is where you will always be received for who you are.

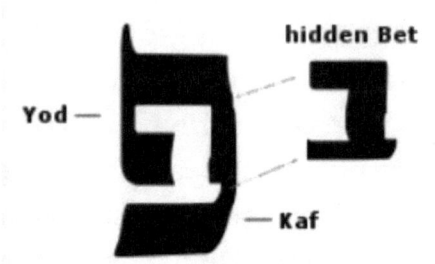

Hebrew for Christians. "The letter Bet/Vet." Last modified 2020.https://hebrew4christians.com/Grammar/Unit_One/Aleph-Bet/bet.html

I am the LORD your God, who brought you up out of Egypt. Open wide your mouth and I will fill it.
Psalm 81:10

Over the course of the next 10 years God is and will be dealing with us as it relates to our mouth in many capacities. Our mouths are to be opened to be fed (receive) the voice of God (be filled with His wisdom for the nation; our family, our friends, our communities, etc.), and as we open wide our mouths toward God, He will fill us with what we need to be sustained in this life. "See how the little birds in their nests seem to be all mouth when the mother comes to feed them. Let it be the same with us. Let us take in grace at every door. Let us drink it in as a sponge sucks up the water in which it lies. God is ready to fill us if we are only ready to be filled."[9]

---

[9] Charles Spurgeon, "Needs to Open Our Mouths," VCY America, September 20, 2020, https://www.vcyamerica.org/charles-spurgeon/2020/09/20/needs-to-open-our-mouths/.

Introduction

Open wide your mouth so God can fill it. "The marvelous promise, 'open thy mouth wide, and I will fill it', has sometimes been used to wrongly justify a lack of preparation, as in, all they have to do is open their mouths and the Lord will give them a message. The true meaning, however, is that If God's people come to Him with great petitions, He will grant them..."[10] God protected the Israelites in the wilderness, he brought them out, and he settled them in the land of Canaan. The Israelites were expected to praise God and to seek Him for the help that they needed instead of turning to other people and places. Life's issues and circumstances can be so overwhelming that it makes us forget what God has previously done for us and others. This causes us to forget to open wide our mouths toward the one who has delivered us before and who can do it again, if we are not intentional about "keeping our minds stayed on Him". Open wide your mouth so God can fill it.

As we have opened our mouths toward God in 2020 the enemy has tried to muzzle our mouths like an ox. Think about it, because of the COVID-19 virus we have had to wear mask since the month of March of 2019 until now as I write this book. Even as we enter into the year 2021/5781, we are still required to wear mask. The enemy has tried to keep our mouths covered as to keep us from receiving what God wants to give us and to silence us from releasing into the atmosphere what God has deposited into

---

[10]"Psalm 81 Explained," Bible Study, last modified 2020, https://wwwbible-studys.org/Bible%20Books/Psalms/Psalm%2081.html.

us. He has tried to muzzle us from communication (prayer) with God about our lives. The enemy has tried to suppress and oppress us with issues and circumstances as a result of COVID-19 with unemployment, deaths, foreclosures, evictions, repossessions, depression, and even quarantine. We have been bound to our homes, causing us to go into quarantine all throughout the entire world. We have been separated from others and restricted to 6ft social distancing. Nonetheless we are still in the decade of The Open Mouth where God is filling us with provision and doing it all while we are in our dwelling places (home). In this season God wants to show up in our homes. We've not had many opportunities to make it to our church buildings and we've had to worship virtually, having to seek (pray and worship) God in our homes with and among our own families. This has given God the opportunity to come into our homes; our places of vulnerability, our place of privacy, our place of comfortability where we are seen and experienced for who we really are without all the frills.

I was recently gifted a pug puppy (Birdie Blu) as an early Christmas gift, and one day when I let her out to relieve herself, I saw one of my childhood friends next door at my neighbor's house. It had been quite some time sense we had seen each other in person. As we exchanged pleasantries, he said to me that he liked the way I looked in my natural state. You see most people only get to see me all dressed up with a fully made-up face, but at home I am dressed relax (with no spanx, lol) and no makeup with only family around to witness. My childhood friend was able to see me in my natural state. In my natural state he was able

Introduction

to see all my flaws that I usually hide from other people. While he appreciated my public self, he said he much more appreciated my natural self. In this season God is wanting to encounter us in our homes in our natural states. With Him we do not have to get all dressed up or made up. He appreciates us for who we are even with our flaws. God wants to minister to our flaws in private. He wants to meet us behind closed doors, in secret without public knowledge, away from observers. Not only does God want to deal with you alone but He wants to deal with your entire family. He wants to heal you and your family too. Open wide the mouth of your home and let God fill the family as a whole.

There is lots of my work that takes place behind closed doors that is not ever seen. —Amal Clooney

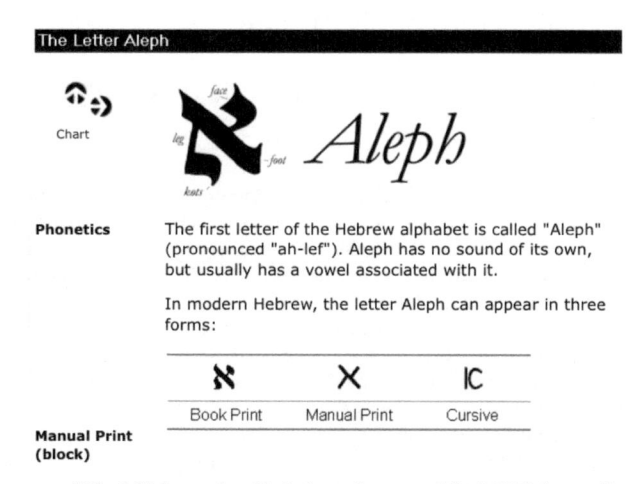

The Letter Aleph

Chart

א *Aleph*
(face, leg, foot, kuts)

Phonetics

The first letter of the Hebrew alphabet is called "Aleph" (pronounced "ah-lef"). Aleph has no sound of its own, but usually has a vowel associated with it.

In modern Hebrew, the letter Aleph can appear in three forms:

א	א	lc
Book Print	Manual Print	Cursive

Manual Print (block)

"The" Hebrew for Christians. Last modified 2020. https://hebrew4christians.com/Grammar/Unit_One/Aleph-Bet/Aleph/aleph.html

As we transition into the year 2021/5781, we are still in the decade of the mouth but in addition we must consider the meaning of the number 1 in the year 5781. The 1 represents the Hebrew letter Aleph. Aleph "(also spelled Alef) is the first letter of the Hebrew alphabet"[11] Aleph represents unity, oneness, primacy, first, and beginning. "The letter Aleph is the 'father' of the Aleph-Beth… it is a silent letter."[12] The symbol for Aleph is the ox or bull which represents strength. The number 1 in 5781 represents unity in quiet strength. Quiet Strength "has a presence that demonstrates both strength and humility at the same time… [it is] described as having this quiet type of strength. People with quiet strength show that they have been tested, have succeeded, and don't need to tell everyone about his or her success."[13] There are many who believe that silence is a sign of weakness. "Silence, although seemingly adverse or even contradictory to [your] cause, is a virtue. Humility is the key."[14]

> *"In quietness and in confidence shall be your strength"*, Isaiah 30:15

---

[11]Kim Engel, "Hebrew Year 5781 (2021 Ad): Aleph in Pey | Silence in the Mouth Part 2," SHEERAH MINISTRIES Waking Eve: Waking Sleeping Beauty, August 8, 2020, https://sheerahministries.com/2020/08/08/hebrew-year-5781-2021-ad-aleph-in-peysilence-in-the-mouth-part2/#:~:text=When%20we%20place%20Aleph%20in,outside%20of%20Jesus%2and%20his.

[12]"The Letter Aleph," Hebrew for Christians, last modified 2020, https://www.hebrew4christians.com/Grammar/Unit_One/Aleph-Bet/Aleph/aleph.html.

[13]Craig Marker, "Quiet Strength: What It Is and What We Can Learn from Those Who Have It," Breaking Muscle, last modified 2020, https://breakingmuscle.com/fitness/quiet-strength-what-it-is-and-what-we-can-learn-from-those-who-have-it#:~:text=He%20or%20she%20has%20a,humility%20at%20the%20same%20time.&text=They%20are%20often%20described%20as,about%20his%2or.

[14]Kim Engel, "Hebrew Year 5781 (2021 Ad): Aleph in Pey | Silence in the Mouth Part 2," SHEERAH MINISTRIES Waking Eve: Waking Sleeping Beauty, August 8, 2020, https://sheerahministries.com/2020/08/08/hebrew-year5781-2021-ad-aleph-in-peysilence-in-the-mouth-part-2/#:~:text=When%20we%20place%20Aleph%20in,outside%20of%20Jesus%20and%20his.

INTRODUCTION

The people of Israel refused to listen to the instructions of God from the prophets and they insisted on doing things their way. The only thing God asks of them was to repent and seek His presence in [quietness] in order to be delivered from defeat at the hands of the Assyrians. God tells them that "In returning and rest shall ye be saved; in quietness and in confidence shall be your strength: and ye would not", (Is 30:15 KJV). Instead of spending time alone with God in [quietness], like the children of Israel, many people would much rather seek the support and wisdom of other people. All God wanted them to do was to come to Him in silence... He wanted them to spend time in His presence. Many of us suffer the silence of God because we refuse to spend time in [quietness].[15]
In quietness you find your confidence and you find your strength.

As we go into the year 2021/5781 it is significant that "we place Aleph in the context of the decade we are in, which we recall is symbolized to us by the Hebrew Letter Pey (a picture symbol of a mouth), then we can see this next year 5781 (September 2020 thru August 2021) has a great deal to do with connecting the dots."[16] The year 2021/5781 is The Year of Quiet Strength. I believe in this decade God wants to deal with us as individuals as it relates to our mouths (our

---

[15]Tammy Isaac, Close the Door: What Happens in the Closet Stays in the Closet (Houston: T.I.M. Publishing, 2019), 45.

[16]Kim Engel, "Hebrew Year 5781 (2021 Ad): Aleph in Pey | Silence in the Mouth Part 2," SHEERAH MINISTRIES Waking Eve: Waking Sleeping Beauty, August 8, 2020, https://sheerahministries.com/2020/08/08/hebrew-year-5781-2021-ad-aleph-in-peysilence-in-the-mouth-part-2/#:~:text=When%20we%20place%20Aleph%20in,outside%20of%20Jesus%20and%20his.

vocalized breath, our organ of speech). He wants to deposit into us His wisdom and knowledge to support, sustained, and strengthen us, and He is doing all this while we are confined (quarantined) to our homes, isolated from people, socially distanced and muzzled (masked when we do go out of our homes).

Not only is God wanting to fill our mouths, but He is also wanting to fill the mouths of our families as we open wide our mouths toward Him. In this decade God wants to heal the family and unify our voices. Without God's voice we do not have a voice of our own. I believe that God is strengthening our voices as we open our mouths (life) toward Him in quietness (prayer). Opening our mouth is about vulnerability, it's about acceptance, it's about faith, it's about willingness, it's about knowing, it is about doing (action), and we do so toward God who is willing and able to do "immeasurably more than all we ask or imagine, according to His power that is at work within us", Ephesians 3:20.

Through our time in prayer God will be unifying the voices of His people so that our reach is extended beyond our comfortable places (homes).

> When we go to God in prayer, we remind ourselves how much we need and depend on Him in our Christian spirituality. Spending time with God in prayer allows believers to develop an intimate relationship with the Father, which equips one to meet life's challenges and struggles. Prayer also allows one to grow spiritually, becoming more

and more like Christ. Without the act of prayer, we would never be able to make it through the many dimensions of life that we face, especially through the dimensions of problems and situations that comes from temptations, trials of our faith, and afflictions. Many of us tend to find prayer challenging because prayer invites us to examine our conscience with regard to all the problems that afflict our lives. At the same time prayer is a way of confronting our life's challenges.[17]

As we open wide our mouths in prayer toward God not only are we inviting God into our circumstances and situations but we are allowing God to unify our voices as a body of Christ so we can all have the same language to fight the good fight of faith.

Quiet, everyone! Shh! Silence before God. Something's afoot in his holy house. He's on the move! Zechariah 2:13 (Message)

In chapter 2 of Zechariah The Prophet instructs the people to quiet (silence) themselves; to be mindful of their conduct, to separate themselves from the wickedness of the world to allow God to move on their behalf. Be quiet because the Lord is in His holy house!" He is not only in his holy house, but he has now raised up; He has moved into action, out of His holy place. In 2021 The Year of Quiet Strength God is calling us to quiet ourselves before Him.

---

[17]Tammy Isaac, Close the Door: What Happens in the Closet Stays in the Closet (Houston: T.I.M. Publishing, 2019), 1.

In our quietness (prayer) before Him we will find our confidence and we will find our strength because God has been moved into action on our behalf.

Contemplative prayer is the discipline of silence in prayer. "The word contemplation had a specific meaning for the first 16 centuries of the Christian era. St. Gregory the Great summed up this meaning at the end of the 6th century as the knowledge of God that is impregnated with love."[18] The contemplative tradition: the prayer-filled life "can show us the way into intimacy with God" …; it is "the human longing for the practice of the presence of God", where we place all our attention on God, "because through it we experience the divine rest that overcomes our alienation"[19], which is the foundation for a lifestyle of holiness, according to Foster, in his book "Streams of Living Water". "Jesus, who retreated often into the rugged wilderness, who lived and worked praying, who heard and did only what the Father said and did, shows forth the contemplative tradition in its fullness and utter beauty."[20] St. John of the Cross once said, "God's first language is silence, and in order to understand [His] language, we must learn to be silent and to rest in God.

Be still and know that I am God; I will be exalted among the nations; I will be exalted in the earth. Psalm 46:10

---

[18] "The Christian Contemplative Tradition," Contemplative Outreach, last modified 2020, https://www.contemplativeoutreach.org/the-christian-contemplative-tradition/.

[19] Richard J. Foster, Streams of Living Water: Celebrating the Great Traditions of Christian Faith. Grand Rapids: HarperOne, 1998.

[20] Ibid

Introduction

As we turn to silence in the presence of God in prayer this year, we should also be prepared to receive God's silence as well. Oswald Chambers says in his book, His "Utmost For His Highest", that "God's silences are His answers. If we only take as answers those that are visible to our senses, we are in a very elementary condition of grace". One Saturday morning I was sitting at home pondering within my heart why God was not speaking to me on a certain matter I had opened my mouth to Him in prayer about. As I sat there it was then that I heard Holy Spirit whisper in my ear saying, "be still and know that I am God". What did He mean, "be still and know"? To "be" is to exist, to occupy a place or position, to continue or remain as before. The word "still" in Hebrew is to cease, abandon, relax, refrain, or to be quiet. God wanted me to be still which meant I needed to continue to exist in a position of relaxation or peace and refrain from anything that would cause me to doubt what God had previously said to me about my life, purpose, and his plan for me as it relates to the situation, I opened my mouth toward about. In addition to being in the position of stillness (quietness) I was to "know", to be aware and acknowledge that He is God. To know that he is the God who" before [I] call [He] will answer; while [I am] still speaking [He] will hear", Isaiah 65:24. To know that he is the God that "when [I] call out to [Him], [He] will answer [me]; [He] will be with [me] in trouble. [He] will deliver and honor [me], Psalm 91:15. To know that he is the God who is willing and able to do "immeasurably more than all we ask or imagine, according to his power that is at work within us", Ephesians 3:20. Acknowledging God implies that we can trust Him and surrender to His plan in the noise of our situation because we know who He is. When God is silent before us, He is trusting us to "be still and know".

Silence puts gaps in conversations, and it can create awkwardness, but the truth is if we listen, we will find that silence communicates much. Silence in some cases can speak much louder than an audible voice. God's silence can be evidence of a growing relationship with Him. At the start of a new relationship there seems to always be something to talk about as you get to know one another. However, in an established relationship where you know one another, there is not much that needs to be spoken and the silence is no longer awkward. The relationship is about just being present (to be still and know), in the silence there is confidence and strengthen.

As you embark upon The Year of Quiet Strength 5781, understand that there is and will continue to be a limit to our interaction and our speaking with those who are not a part of our household. Know that God is unifying and strengthening (healing) our voices as families as we spend time in our own homes. He is also unifying and strengthening our voices as a body of believers as we meet with Him in prayer (quietness) and open wide our mouth toward Him. Opening our mouths is about spending time with God in our places of vulnerability, our place of privacy, our place of comfortability where we are seen and experienced for who we really are without all the frills. Opening our mouths toward God is about openness, it's about acceptance, it's about faith, it's about willingness,

Introduction

it's about knowing, it is about doing (action), and we do so toward God who is willing and able to do "immeasurably more than all we ask or imagine, according to His power that is at work within us", Ephesians 3:20. Opening our mouths toward God is about meeting God in the stillness of prayer and allowing Him to give us unified confidence and strength as His people.

HOW TO PRAY THIS BOOK

Greetings, and thank you for purchasing this book and trusting me to take you on a 31-day journey focusing on our mouths as we are in the decade of The Open Mouth. The purpose of the book is to help you understand the season that we are in and to help you understand how to navigate through these times of unfamiliarity and uncertainty rather than adjust to a "new normal" because of COVID-19. I am surprised at how many people have settled for a "new normal" rather than looking at it as a temporary season that shall pass as many stressful seasons has, though as traumatic as they have been.

This book is an invitation to journey with me as we together open our mouths toward God in daily scripture reading and contemplative prayer. This is not just another book to read swiftly through, it is an invitation to practice spiritual disciplines. This book is about helping you to see that you are not confined or restricted but that you are free, your spirit is free to rest in the silence of God and know that God is God.

It is ideal to move through the book day-by-day (from day 1 to day 31). However, this 31-day journey is not about binding you to a strict schedule. If you miss a day pick back up the next day. If you feel you need to spend more time on a particular day, then do so in order to discern what Holy Spirit wants you to discover. Or if you feel like a day does not resonate with you then move to the next day but be sure you listen to Holy Spirit before you do so.

Take your time, read slowly and purposefully as this is meant to be a contemplative experience. "Contemplative prayer begins with "centering prayer," a meditative practice where the practitioner [you] focuses on a word [or phrase] and repeats that word [or phrase] over and over for the duration of the exercise. The purpose is to clear one's mind of outside concerns so that God's voice may be more easily heard. After the centering prayer, the practitioner [you are] to sit still, listen for direct guidance from God, and feel His presence."[1] Contemplation is like mediation but unlike meditation, the goal is to have the mind at a resting state in the presence of God which allows us to absorb in God's love for us.

Each day as you begin make sure to create a sacred space to read the daily scripture, make a declaration, and spend time in contemplative prayer. It is suggested that you set aside a minimum of 10 minutes daily to experience the daily devotional. Below you will find instructions on how to create a sacred space taken from my previous book on prayer titled Close The

---

[1] "What Is Contemplative Prayer?," Got Questions, last modified 2020, https://www.gotquestions.org/contemplative-prayer.html.

Door. Each day you are given a scripture to read, a declaration to declare and a prayer to pray. You will also be given space to write what you discern Holy Spirit is saying to you at the time.

HOW TO CREATE A SACRED SPACE

1. Designate a space, room, or closet in your home or office. You may want to furnish it with a chair, table, a lamp, a notebook, a bible, a prayer shawl, a pillow, etc.…

2. Schedule a time. It may help if you set a regular time for when you will spend time with God. As you become more consistent in spending time with God in prayer you will not only have a regular scheduled time, but you will begin to sense when God is calling you to a time of prayer alone with Him.

3. Get in there. Be intentional about utilizing the space.

4. Sit still and quiet. Center yourself by quoting a word or phrase to still your thoughts.

5. Keep the space sacred. The only thing done in that space should be prayer.[1]

---

[1] Tammy Isaac, Close the Door: What Happens in the Closet Stays in the Closet (Houston: T.I.M. Publishing, 2019), 76.

THIRTY ONE DAYS WITH *TAMMY M. ISAAC, MDIV.*

DAY 1

SCRIPTURE:
May these words of my mouth and this meditation of my heart be pleasing in your sight, Lord, my Rock and my Redeemer.
Psalm 19:14

PRAYER:
Father, I know that everything that I say, and think is not always pleasing to you. However, it is my heart's desire that you would take pleasure in all that I am. Today, I ask that you forgive me for speech that is degrading of myself and others and that you forgive me of thoughts that are unacceptable to you. Father, you are my rock and redeemer, let everything that flows from my mouth and heart agree with and be acceptable to You today.
In Jesus Name, Amen.

PERSONAL PRAYER:

_____

_____

CENTERING PRAYER PHRASE:
My mind and heart belong to God

DECLARE THROUGHOUT THE DAY:
I speak and think of only things that is pleasing to God.

What is Holy Spirit saying to you in this moment?

_____

_____

_____

DAY 2

SCRIPTURE:

I will raise up for them a prophet like you from among their fellow Israelites, and I will put my words in his mouth. He will tell them everything I command him. Deuteronomy 18:18

PRAYER:

Father, I thank you for choosing to trust me with your words when you could have chosen someone else. I open my mouth toward you this day that you may put your words in me. Everything that I speak will be only what you have given me to speak. Thank you that those you place in my sphere to influence with your words will receive me as one who spends time with you and speaks for you. In Jesus Name, Amen.

PERSONAL PRAYER:

_____

_____

CENTERING PRAYER PHRASE:

I speak for God.

DECLARE THROUGHOUT THE DAY:

My speech toward others has been divinely orchestrated by God.

What is Holy Spirit saying to you in this moment?

_____

_____

DAY 3

SCRIPTURE:
No, the word is very near you; it is in your mouth and in your heart so you may obey it. Deuteronomy 30:14

PRAYER:
Father, I thank you for letting me know that your word is never too far away from me. I am grateful to you for placing your word in my mouth and my heart. For it's your word that helps me to be obedient to you. Thank you that your word will never lead me astray from your will. In Jesus Name, Amen.

PERSONAL PRAYER:

_____

_____

CENTERING PRAYER PHRASE:
God's word is in my mouth.

DECLARE THROUGHOUT THE DAY:
I obey God because His word is rooted on the inside of me.

What is Holy Spirit saying to you in this moment?

_____

_____

DAY 4

SCRIPTURE:
Keep this Book of the Law always on your lips; meditate on it day and night, so that you may be careful to do everything written in it. Then you will be prosperous and successful.
Joshua 1:8

PRAYER:
Father, I pray that before I speak a word in distress, you would cause the meditated Word in my spirit to counterattack any emotional speech that would prevent me from being prosperous and successful. May I spend ample time reading your word with understand that it will not depart from your written word. In Jesus Name, Amen.

PERSONAL PRAYER:

_____

_____

CENTERING PRAYER PHRASE:
I speak prosperity and success.

DECLARE THROUGHOUT THE DAY:
I don't speak out of my emotions I speak from the meditated word of God that's in my mouth.

What is Holy Spirit saying to you in this moment?

_____

_____

DAY 5

SCRIPTURE:
But my mouth would encourage you; comfort from my lips would bring you relief. Job 16:5

PRAYER:
Father, in this season where there is so many people grieving, I pray that there are words of encouragement in my mouth to comfort those who need relief from life's troubles and situations. Forgive me if my words have brought anything but comfort to those hurting. Father, daily may I strategically be placed among those whom I can comfort with my words. In Jesus Name, Amen.

PERSONAL PRAYER:

_____

_____

CENTERING PRAYER PHRASE:
My words are comforting.

DECLARE THROUGHOUT THE DAY:
Daily my words bring encouragement to those who need relief.

What is Holy Spirit saying to you in this moment?

_____

_____

DAY 6

SCRIPTURE:
Do not keep talking so proudly or let your mouth speak such arrogance, for the LORD is a God who knows, and by him deeds are weighed. 1 Samuel 2:3

PRAYER:
Father, I pray for a humble mouth. One that is reserved not to speak prideful. I submit my speech to the will of God that He may navigate how and when I speak. Help me to be mindful that the Lord is always listening to what I speak.
In Jesus Name, Amen.

PERSONAL PRAYER:

_____

_____

CENTERING PRAYER PHRASE:
Pride is not my portion.

DECLARE THROUGHOUT THE DAY:
Humility is shown through my speech because I am not proud or arrogant.

What is Holy Spirit saying to you in this moment?

_____

_____

DAY 7

SCRIPTURE:
Lord, who may dwell in your sacred tent? Who may live on your holy mountain? The one whose walk is blameless, who does what is righteous, who speaks the truth from their heart; whose tongue utters no slander, who does no wrong to a neighbor, and casts no slur on others; Psalm 15:1-3

PRAYER:
Father, I pray to be able to dwell in your presence. I pray to make your sanctuary and holy hill my dwelling place. May I be found blameless and doing what is always righteous. Help me not to speak slander against my neighbor but let my tongue speak truth from your heart. In Jesus Name, Amen.

PERSONAL PRAYER:

_____

_____

CENTERING PRAYER PHRASE:
My tongue speaks truth.

DECLARE THROUGHOUT THE DAY:
I walk blameless and do what is righteous therefore I dwell in God's presence.

What is Holy Spirit saying to you in this moment?

_____

_____

_____

DAY 8

SCRIPTURE:
But the things that come out of a person's mouth come from the heart, and these defile them. Matthew 15:18

PRAYER:
Father create in me a clean heart. Purge me from all unrighteousness. Search my heart and see if there be anything in me that would cause my mouth to speak unclean things. In Jesus Name, Amen.

PERSONAL PRAYER:

_____

_____

CENTERING PRAYER PHRASE:
My heart is pure.

DECLARE THROUGHOUT THE DAY:
I have a renewed heart and pure clean washed spirit.

What is Holy Spirit saying to you in this moment?

_____

_____

DAY 9

SCRIPTURE:
After I had spoken, they spoke no more; my words fell gently on their ears. They waited for me as for showers and drank in my words as the spring rain, Job 29:22-23

PRAYER:
Father I have no voice without your voice, so I intentionally sit in your presence to hear from you. Like the dew in the morning let your word gently rest upon me. In Jesus Name, Amen.

PERSONAL PRAYER:

_____

_____

CENTERING PRAYER PHRASE:
God's word quenches my thirst.

DECLARE THROUGHOUT THE DAY:
I wait daily to hear the voice of God to rest upon me like the dew in the morning.

What is Holy Spirit saying to you in this moment?

_____

_____

DAY 10

SCRIPTURE:

Call on me in the day of trouble; I will deliver you, and you will honor me. Psalm 50:15

PRAYER:
Father by my own confession, cause me to be slow to speak and anger so that my mouth may not testify against me or bring judgment down on my own head. In Jesus Name, Amen.

PERSONAL PRAYER:

_____

_____

CENTERING PRAYER PHRASE:
God is my deliverer.

DECLARE THROUGHOUT THE DAY:
Every time I called on God, He delivered me.

What is Holy Spirit saying to you in this moment?

_____

_____

The mouth is an external opening which is the expression of the breath and through our mouths our breath becomes vocalized.

OPEN WIDE YOUR MOUTH

Growing up in Houston, TX during the 1980's one of the most popular places to go as a child on the weekends, or during a school break, was Six Flags AstroWorld amusement park. If you are over the age 40 you probably know the place that I am talking about, and you have possibly been there before. I can remember as a kid, my friends and I would sometimes get dropped off early in the morning around 8am at the amusement park. There we would wait outside the park's gate for them to open at 10am, with our $5 off empty coke can for the price of admission into the park.

> AstroWorld, was a seasonally operated amusement park located in Houston, Texas. Owned and operated by Six Flags. The park opened on June 1, 1968 and was originally developed and constructed as part of the Astrodomain, the brainchild of local philanthropist and former Houston mayor Roy Hofheinz, who intended it to complement the Astrodome.

AstroWorld, was a seasonally operated amusement park. It featured various rides and games, as well as other events for entertainment purposes. There were also summer concerts and 4th of July fireworks. During the Christmas break AstroWorld would be turned into a winter wonderland with decorations and holiday shows. The rides, the entertainment and the concerts created a lifetime of memories for children, their families, and their friends. AstroWorld was a child's dream and one of the coolest places to hang out. However, for me it was more like a nightmare to be honest. Well, at least the rollercoasters were. I particularly was not as excited as my peers to go to AstroWorld and ride the rollercoasters. The reason was because I had a fear of riding rollercoasters.

AstroWorld had six rollercoasters with an average wait time of 45 minutes each on busy days. The scariest rollercoaster to me was the 60-mile-per-hour Texas Cyclone, an old-fashioned wooden replica of Coney Island's famous Cyclone. The Texas Cyclone was "well-known for its airtime, the roller coaster was 93 feet (28 m) tall, 3,180 feet (970 m) long, and had a ride time of two minutes and fifteen seconds".[1] When it first opened, it was one of the tallest and fastest wooden rollercoasters in the world. Whenever I would go to AstroWorld with my school, church, or family, I would play games but never ride any of the rollercoasters, especially the Texas Cyclone. I would stand in line with my friends until it was time for them to get on the rollercoaster and then I would walk around to the exit of the ride to meet them there when they exited the ride.

By the time I made it to high school AstroWorld was still an extremely popular place to go, even on field trips. When I was in the 9th grade, I was a part of a program called Upward Bound at Texas Southern University (TSU). The Upward Bound program

---

[1] "Texas Cyclone," Wikipedi The Free Encyclopedia, July 22, 2020, https:/en.wikipedia.org/wiki/Texas_Cyclone.

> *I was nervous and scared straight but I got on the ride anyway. All the while I was thinking "what are you doing girl!"*

provided "fundamental support to participants in their preparation for college entrance"[2], and one year the program took a group of us on a fieldtrip to AstroWorld as a reward for our good work on our schoolwork. Everybody was excited about the trip and they all raved about how they were going to ride the Texas Cyclone. As I normally would whenever I went to AstroWorld with my friends, I walked with the other students to the ride waited in line with them and when it was almost time for them to get on the ride, I told them that I would meet them at the exit of the ride. But they would not have it. They peer pressured me into getting on the ride. I was nervous and scared straight but I got on the ride anyway. All the while I was thinking "what are you doing girl, you have nothing to prove to them, don't get on the ride".

> *To scream is to utter a loud, piercing cry, especially of pain, fear, anger, or excitement".*

Not wanting to look like a wimp, I got into the seat of the rollercoaster and buckled the seatbelt as tight as I could and began to pray "Lord, Keep Me". As the ride began to move, it moved slowly building momentum to a fast, faster, and an even faster speed, so fast that the wind slammed me back, making me one with the seat and I opened wide my mouth and I screamed for dear life. I mean, I screamed and screamed and screamed.

---

[2] "About Upward Bound," Texas Southern University, last modified 2020, http://tsu.edu/students-services/departments/trio/upward-bound/about-upward-bound.html.

While some people remained silent with their eyes closed, and others were laughing like they were not even scared. I opened wide my mouth and I screamed. I remember having my hair pulled back into a ball with a fake hair piece attached to it to make a hair bun. In those days we did not have premade buns like we do now. We had to take braiding hair and braid it and then wrap it around our real hair to create a bun. Well, when the ride was over, I was so relieved to be exiting the ride that I never even noticed that my hair bun was missing until all my friends started asking me "where is your bun". I screamed one more time, this time because I was embarrassed.

I screamed! "To scream is to utter a loud, piercing cry, especially of pain, fear, anger, or excitement".[3] Emory psychologist Harold Gouzoules who studies human screams, "found that people can distinguish different types of screams: A happy scream, a frightened scream, a scream given in pain."[4] There are several reasons why a person would scream. However, it was because of my fear that I opened wide my mouth and I screamed as loud as I could while riding the rollercoaster. Gouzoules goes on to say that "The ability to belt out a scream is deeply rooted in our evolutionary history, and is no doubt critical to our survival, he says, screams communicate to the screamer's nearby relatives and allies whether it's a serious fight,

---

[3] "Scream," Dictionary.com, last modified 2020, https://www.dictionary.com/browse/scream.

[4] Carol Clark, "The Psychology of Screams," Emory News Center, last modified October 18, 2013, https://news.emory.edu/stories/2013/10/esc_psychology_of_a_scream/campus.html.

requiring their assistance, or just a minor squabble."[5] My screaming was communicating to others around me that I was afraid. It communicated that I was not enjoying the ride at all and that I wanted to be let off the ride. I was so overwhelmed with fear that

> "The ability to belt out a scream is deeply rooted in our evolutionary history, and is no doubt critical to our survival, he says, screams communicate to the screamer's nearby relatives and allies whether it's a serious fight, requiring their assistance, or just a minor squabble.
>
> —Harold Gouzoules

I did not care who heard me screaming or what anyone else thought about me.

I am reminded of the Jonathan McReynolds' 2018 third studio album titled Make Room. It earned McReynolds two Grammy nominations, a nomination for Best Gospel Album, nine Stellar Award nominations eight of which he won. On the Make Room album McReynolds has an interlude titled Rollercoasters where he talks about his own experience while riding rollercoasters and people's responses to them. He says,

> If you go to an amusement park, look at the rollercoasters. There are two types of rollercoaster riders. There [is] one like me, who's very quiet. Holds on to the bar real tight. And then you have another one. They just throw up their hands and scream, "AHH". The weird part about it is [the one like] me.

---

[5] Carol Clark, "The Psychology of Screams," Emory News Center, last modified October 18, 2013, https://news.emory.edu/stories/2013/10/esc_psychology_of_a_scream/campus.html.

Who [is] sitting there, tryin' to be all cool about it. And I [am] holding everything in. I [am] feeling all those drops more than the people that have their hands up [screaming]. And it just seems like in this season. It just seems like God is purposely putting me through a little bit of [a] rollercoaster action. Some rises and some falls to see if for once if I would just "Ah!", Jesus, Jesus, I can't do this by myself.[6]

Then McReynolds begins to sing "There is power in the name of Jesus". What he is wanting us to understand is that in the rising and the falling of our lives (rollercoaster action) we should be calling on the name of Jesus. Many times, life can be like a rollercoaster rising and falling just as fast as the Texas Cyclone and instead of riding this rollercoaster called life like we have it all together we should simply open wide

> *Your scream is a prayer that communicates to God that you need His help! Your screams communicating to God that your dependency is upon Him. Your scream communicates to God your vulnerability and willingness to confess that you can't take this ride alone.*

our mouths and call on The Lord who is our present help. Your scream is a prayer that communicates to God that you need His help! Your screams communicating to God that your dependency is upon Him. Your scream communicates to God your vulnerability and willingness to confess that you cannot take this ride alone. This rollercoaster life that you are on, you do not have to be on alone. You do not have to take life's ride in so much pride and self-strength that

---

[6]"L.R.F. (Rollercoasters) Lyrics," Genius, last modified 2013, https://genius.com/Jonathan-mcreynolds-lrf-rollercoasters-lyrics.

you really do not even have. God wants to walk with you through your journey, and there are people who wants to pray with you through your journey and encourage you. Lift your hands and OPEN WIDE YOUR MOUTH!

Lift your hands and
OPEN WIDE YOUR MOUTH!

DAY 11

SCRIPTURE:
My dear brothers, take note of this: Everyone should be quick to listen, slow to speak and slow to become angry, for man's anger does not bring about the righteous life that God desires. James 1:19-20

PRAYER:
Father, I do not want to be one who does not listen. Help me to be opened to hear from other people. I pray that I take time to review a thing and consult with you before I speak quickly in anger. I pray to have spirit-led actions that will allow Holy Spirit to act for me instead of me reacting so that it will insure my righteousness in you. In Jesus Name, Amen.

PERSONAL PRAYER:

_____

_____

CENTERING PRAYER PHRASE:
I am quick to listen and slow to speak.

DECLARE THROUGHOUT THE DAY:
My speech brings about the righteous life that God desires.

What is Holy Spirit saying to you in this moment?

DAY 12

SCRIPTURE:
The words of the reckless pierce like swords, but the tongue of the wise brings healing. Proverbs 12:18

PRAYER:
Father reverse the effects of pierced words spoken and rid the atmosphere of them that were spoken to me and by me. God forgive me for using my words to hurt others. I pray my words will not be reckless, let them be full of healing, comfort, and peace. In Jesus Name, Amen.

PERSONAL PRAYER:

_____

_____

CENTERING PRAYER PHRASE:
My words are healing.

DECLARE THROUGHOUT THE DAY:
I will not use my words to be reckless, rather they will bring to this nation.

What is Holy Spirit saying to you in this moment?

_____

_____

DAY 13

SCRIPTURE:
Those who guard their lips preserve their lives, but those who speak rashly will come to ruin. Proverbs 13:3

PRAYER:
Father help me keep my lips from speaking words that shortens my life. I do not want to speak hastily in the moment and destroy relationship or deter blessings you have set up for me. Let the words I speak out of my mouth be a preserver of life. In Jesus Name, Amen.

PERSONAL PRAYER:

_____

_____

CENTERING PRAYER PHRASE:
God preserve my speech.

DECLARE THROUGHOUT THE DAY:
I do not speak rashly; I speak words that preserves my life and others.

What is Holy Spirit saying to you in this moment?

_____

_____

DAY 14

SCRIPTURE:
He will yet fill your mouth with laughter and your lips with shouts of joy. Job 8:21

PRAYER:
Father cause me to meditate on and be conscious of the power and position of my mouth. God make me laugh again turn my frown into a smile. Let my mouth be filled with laughter and my lips with shouts of joy. In Jesus Name, In Jesus Name, Amen.

PERSONAL PRAYER:

_____

_____

CENTERING PRAYER PHRASE:
Laughter and shouts of joy are in my mouth.

DECLARE THROUGHOUT THE DAY:
My mouth will be filled with laughter and shots of joy all my days.

What is Holy Spirit saying to you in this moment?

_____

_____

DAY 15

SCRIPTURE:
He saves the needy from the sword in their mouth; he saves them from the clutches of the powerful. Job 5:15

PRAYER:
*Father have mercy on me and save me from the sword in my mouth. When I am in need let me not become discourage and speak negatively about my situation. Help me to hold fast to the confession of my faith. Remind me that you are my provider and sustainer.
In Jesus Name, Amen.*

PERSONAL PRAYER:

_____

_____

CENTERING PRAYER PHRASE:
God is my provider and sustainer.

DECLARE THROUGHOUT THE DAY:
My God is more powerful than any situation I am in.

What is Holy Spirit saying to you in this moment?

_____

_____

DAY 16

SCRIPTURE:

When we put bits into the mouths of horses to make them obey us, we can turn the whole animal. Or take ships as an example. Although they are so large and are driven by strong winds, they are steered by a very small rudder wherever the pilot wants to go. Likewise, the tongue is a small part of the body, but it makes great boasts. Consider what a great forest is set on fire by a small spark. The tongue also is a fire, a world of evil among the parts of the body. It corrupts the whole body, sets the whole course of one's life on fire, and is itself set on fire by hell. All kinds of animals, birds, reptiles and sea creatures are being tamed and have been tamed by mankind, but no human being can tame the tongue. It is a restless evil, full of deadly poison. With the tongue we praise our Lord and Father, and with it we curse human beings, who have been made in God's likeness. Out of the same mouth come praise and cursing. My brothers and sisters, this should not be. Can both fresh water and salt water flow from the same spring? James 3:3-11

PRAYER:

*Father, I pray that I understand how deadly my tongue can be if there is not a taming of it. Help me to take responsibility for my words and the words that are framed in my thoughts before they flow out of my mouth.
In Jesus Name, Amen.*

PERSONAL PRAYER:

_____

_____

CENTERING PRAYER PHRASE:

God tame my tongue.

OPEN WIDE YOUR MOUTH

DECLARE THROUGHOUT THE DAY:

Out of my mouth flow blessings not cursings.

What is Holy Spirit saying to you in this moment?

_____

_____

DAY 17

SCRIPTURE:
Let your conversation be always full of grace, seasoned with salt, so that you may know how to answer everyone. Colossians 4:6

PRAYER:
Father let my conversations be stimulated by God's grace and marked by wisdom that I may be able answer every person appropriately.
In Jesus Name, Amen.

PERSONAL PRAYER:

_____

_____

CENTERING PRAYER PHRASE:
God grace my speech.

DECLARE THROUGHOUT THE DAY:
Daily my conversations are filled with God's grace.

What is Holy Spirit saying to you in this moment?

_____

_____

DAY 18

SCRIPTURE:
Words from the mouth of the wise are gracious, but fools are consumed by their own lips. Ecclesiastes 10:12

PRAYER:
Father I do not want to be looked upon as a fool whose words destroy them. I pray that the words that flow through my mouth are gracious and are wise. In Jesus Name, Amen.

PERSONAL PRAYER:

_____

_____

CENTERING PRAYER PHRASE:
My words are gracious.

DECLARE THROUGHOUT THE DAY:
I no longer speak words to destroy myself and others, my words are gracious.

What is Holy Spirit saying to you in this moment?

_____

_____

DAY 19

SCRIPTURE:

Let the message of Christ dwell among you richly as you teach and admonish one another with all wisdom through psalms, hymns, and songs from the Spirit, singing to God with gratitude in your hearts.

Colossians 3:16

PRAYER:

Father may the words that Christ speaks dwell within me richly in all wisdom. Let His words be my words that I may teach and admonish those around me with psalms and hymns and spiritual songs, singing with grace in my heart. In Jesus Name, Amen.

PERSONAL PRAYER:

_____

_____

CENTERING PRAYER PHRASE:

Christ words dwell in me.

DECLARE THROUGHOUT THE DAY:

I influence those around me with the words of Christ that dwells inside of me.

What is Holy Spirit saying to you in this moment?

_____

_____

DAY 20

SCRIPTURE:
Those who guard their mouths and their tongues keep themselves from calamity. Proverbs 21:23

PRAYER:
Father teach me to keep watch over the words that comes out of my mouth and help me to keep my soul from experiencing trouble. Help me to live a life of peace and I speak into the atmosphere. Let my words bring peace to the life others. I pray my life prospers even as my soul prospers.
In Jesus Name, Amen.

PERSONAL PRAYER:

CENTERING PRAYER PHRASE:
God keep watch over my mouth.

DECLARE THROUGHOUT THE DAY:
My words prosper my soul and brings peace to my life.

What is Holy Spirit saying to you in this moment?

Unfortunately, we tend to blame others when do not get what we seek to attain. Yet the truth is that we have not opened our mouths.

A CLOSED MOUTH DON'T GET FED

One Saturday morning as I was scrolling through Facebook, I noticed that one of my Facebook friends posted a message that there was a single young mother she knew, who was expecting twin boys any day now, and was in need. My Facebook friend was gathering gently used items and needed them to be donated by the next day.

Four hours later my Facebook friend posted another message. Her post read: "When I tell you God is Good!!! You better believe it." She wrote "my phone has not stop ringing since I made the post this morning about the mother-to-be who is in need! The donations are overflowing, and I am so GRATEFUL!" She goes on to state that "the moral of the story is 'don't let your pride keep you in your struggle'". In other words what she was saying is that "A Closed Mouth Don't Get Fed". I am sure you have heard the saying before. It means that unless you open your mouth and communicate what you need, then you will not get that which you need. What is it that you need today? What is it that you have been hesitant to speak about? What is it that you are afraid of? Simon Placr writes in an article titled Closed Mouths Don't Get Fed: The Power of Asking for What You Want,

> One thing I have discovered that helps a lot: coming to the realization that getting a "no," versus "not asking," produces the same result. For example: there's a big summer internship that has a difficult application process. Sure, the application process seems daunting, and you may be nervous. But guess what? If you don't apply, you get the same exact outcome as if you do apply and get rejected. The only difference is, in the first scenario, you're left forever wondering what could have been.[1]

Placr suggests to us that it is important that we learn to open our mouths and let God and those around us know what we need. But if by chance that we are told "no" or "not right now," we can still move forward. "Having the courage and determination to face your fears and ask for what you want, when you want it, (even if the answer is sometimes "no,") will only ever open more doors than it closes. That, I can guarantee."[2]

If we are honest many of us need something even now and we have gone without because we have not had the courage to open our mouths. When we do not open our mouths to communication our needs, they go unannounced and we become content in our lack. Unfortunately, we tend to blame others when do not get what we seek to attain. Yet

---

[1] Simon Placr, "Closed Mouths Don't Get Fed: The Power of Asking for What You Want," Her Campus at Murray State, May 8, 2018, https://www.hercampus.com/school/murray-state/closed-mouths-dont-get-fed-power-asking-what-you-want.

[2] Ibid.

the truth is that we have not opened our mouths "I will answer them before they even call to me. While they are still talking about their

> *When we do not open our mouths to communication our needs, they go unannounced and we become content in our lack.*

needs, I will go ahead and answer their prayers, Isaiah 65:24!" God knows what we desire, and he has it already to give to us. Closed Mouths Don't Get Fed.

DAY 21

SCRIPTURE:
The tongue has the power of life and death, and those who love it will eat its fruit. Proverbs 18:21

PRAYER:
Father I pray that each time that I open my mouth I speak life. Help me to be mindful of what I say, before I say it. It is not my intention to speak death over myself or anyone else. I love to speak life.
In Jesus Name, Amen.

PERSONAL PRAYER:

_____

_____

CENTERING PRAYER PHRASE:
Lord let my words bring life.

DECLARE THROUGHOUT THE DAY:
When I open my mouth to speak, I bring life to all.

What is Holy Spirit saying to you in this moment?

_____

_____

DAY 22

SCRIPTURE:
Whoever believes in me, as Scripture has said, rivers of living water will flow from within them. John 7:38

PRAYER:
Father, I believe in you and your word just as the scripture said. Now let your Holy Spirit move through me as you see fit. I give Holy Spirit full access to me. Let your word flow out of my mouth life a river running down stream. In Jesus Name, Amen.

PERSONAL PRAYER:

_____

_____

CENTERING PRAYER PHRASE:
Holy Spirit flow through me.

DECLARE THROUGHOUT THE DAY:
When I open my mouth to speak Holy Spirit flows through me.

What is Holy Spirit saying to you in this moment?

_____

_____

DAY 23

SCRIPTURE:
A good man brings good things out of the good stored up in his heart, and an evil man brings evil things out of the evil stored up in his heart. For the mouth speaks what the heart is full of. Luke 6:45

PRAYER:
Father let me be found as good in your sight that goodness may be brought forth from my heart. Anything in my heart that would cause bitterness, resentment, anger or the likes please heal me that no evil can flow from my heart. Let my heart be filled and overflowing with love that my speech may reflect the love of God. In Jesus Name, Amen.

PERSONAL PRAYER:

_____

_____

CENTERING PRAYER PHRASE:
Goodness is in my heart.

DECLARE THROUGHOUT THE DAY:
My heart bears the fruit of goodness and so does my speech.

What is Holy Spirit saying to you in this moment?

_____

_____

_____

DAY 24

SCRIPTURE:
His talk is smooth as butter, yet war is in his heart; his words are more soothing than oil, yet they are drawn swords. Psalm 55:21

PRAYER:
Father may my heart and my mouth both line up with your love. I pray that my heart is overfilled with the love of God and my speech reflects that same love. Let there not be a conflict between my heart and my words.
In Jesus Name, Amen.

PERSONAL PRAYER:

_____

_____

CENTERING PRAYER PHRASE:
My heart and my mouth both speak love.

DECLARE THROUGHOUT THE DAY:
My heart and my mouth are both lined up with the love of God.

What is Holy Spirit saying to you in this moment?

_____

_____

DAY 25

SCRIPTURE:
My mouth is filled with your praise, declaring your splendor all day long. Psalm 71:8

PRAYER:
Father may my mouth be always filled with praise and honor unto you. I pray that no day passes by without me lifting your name vocally. It brings me much delight speak of your goodness all day long. In Jesus Name, Amen.

PERSONAL PRAYER:

_____

_____

CENTERING PRAYER PHRASE:
I honor and praise you God.

DECLARE THROUGHOUT THE DAY:
My mouth is filled with praise and honor for God.

What is Holy Spirit saying to you in this moment?

_____

_____

DAY 26

SCRIPTURE:
Then the woman said to Elijah, "Now I know that you are a man of God and that the word of the Lord from your mouth is the truth. 1 Kings 17:24

PRAYER:
Father when I speak, I pray that people will know that I am a child of God. May I be known as one who speaks truth. I pray my reputation of truth precedes me. In Jesus Name, Amen.

PERSONAL PRAYER:

_____

_____

CENTERING PRAYER PHRASE:
I am a child of God.

DECLARE THROUGHOUT THE DAY:
I consistently speak the truth of God.

What is Holy Spirit saying to you in this moment?

_____

_____

DAY 27

SCRIPTURE:
True instruction was in his mouth and nothing false was found on his lips. He walked with me in peace and uprightness and turned many from sin. Malachi 2:6, 7

PRAYER:
Father, I pray that truth is in my mouth and no iniquity is found on my lips. With my mouth I turn others away from iniquity and I set an example of walking in peace and uprightness. Let my mouth be filled with knowledge and let it flow from my lips. In Jesus Name, Amen.

PERSONAL PRAYER:

_____

_____

CENTERING PRAYER PHRASE:
Truth is on my lips.

DECLARE THROUGHOUT THE DAY:
My truthful, peaceful, and uprightness brings me peace and influences others.

What is Holy Spirit saying to you in this moment?

_____

_____

_____

DAY 28

SCRIPTURE:

Well, I have come to you now," Balaam replied. "But I can't say whatever I please. I must speak only what God puts in my mouth.
Numbers 22:38

PRAYER:

Father, I only want to speak that which you place in my mouth. If you have not given me the authority to speak let me not speak. If I have not heard from you let me not speak. Let everything I speak be with the power and permission of you. In Jesus Name, Amen.

PERSONAL PRAYER:

_____

_____

CENTERING PRAYER PHRASE:

God's word is in my mouth.

DECLARE THROUGHOUT THE DAY:

I speak with the power and the permission of God.

What is Holy Spirit saying to you in this moment?

DAY 29

SCRIPTURE:

I have much to say in judgment of you. But he who sent me is trustworthy, and what I have heard from him I tell the world." They did not understand that he was telling them about his Father. So Jesus said, "When you have lifted up the Son of Man, then you will know that I am he and that I do nothing on my own but speak just what the Father has taught me.
John 8:26-28

PRAYER:

Father, I pray that I would speak only that which I have learned and heard from you. Father no matter what I may feel I need to say and or judge, I will not do so without you instructing me to do so.
In Jesus Name, Amen.

PERSONAL PRAYER:

_____

_____

CENTERING PRAYER PHRASE:
My speech is instructed by God.

DECLARE THROUGHOUT THE DAY:
Without the instruction of God himself, I deny myself the right to speak on my own.

What is Holy Spirit saying to you in this moment?

_____

_____

_____

DAY 30

SCRIPTURE:
Now the evening before the man arrived, the hand of the Lord was on me, and he opened my mouth before the man came to me in the morning. So my mouth was opened and I was no longer silent.
Ezekiel 33:22

PRAYER:
Father I pray that you strengthen my voice and give me the ability to speak in the face of adversity. Lord do not allow my voice to be taken away from me or let me remain silent when my voice is needed. In Jesus Name, Amen.

PERSONAL PRAYER:

_____

_____

CENTERING PRAYER PHRASE:
God open my mouth and speak through me.

DECLARE THROUGHOUT THE DAY:
I will not be silent when my voice needs to be heard.

What is Holy Spirit saying to you in this moment?

_____

_____

DAY 31

SCRIPTURE:
My inmost being will rejoice when your lips speak what is right. Proverbs 23:16

PRAYER:
Father I pray that I always speak in a manner that pleases you. That I speak to people in ways that make them feel good about themselves. Father let my thoughts be full of joy as I speak in a proper manner.
In Jesus Name, Amen.

PERSONAL PRAYER:

_____

_____

CENTERING PRAYER PHRASE:
My thoughts are full of joy.

DECLARE THROUGHOUT THE DAY:
My thoughts are full of joy as I speak in a proper manner.

What is Holy Spirit saying to you in this moment?

_____

_____

Bibliography

Bible Study. "Psalm 81 Explained." Last modified 2020. https://www.bible-studys.org/Bible%20Books/Psalms/Psalm%2081.html.

Chabad. "The Hebrew Alphabet." Last modified 2020. https://www.chabad.org/library/article_cdo/aid/4069287/jewish/The-Hebrew-Alphabet.htm.

Clark, Carol. "The Psychology of Screams." Emory News Center. Last modified October 18, 2013. https://news.emory.edu/stories/2013/10/esc_psychology_of_a_scream/campus.html

Contemplative Outreach. "The Christian Contemplative Tradition." Last modified 2020. https://www.contemplativeoutreach.org/the-christian-contemplative-tradition/.

Dictionary.com. "Scream." Last modified 2020. https://www.dictionary.com/browse/scream.

Engel, Kim. "Hebrew Year 5781 (2021 Ad):Aleph in Pey Ι Silence in the Mouth Part 2." SHEERAH MINISTRIES Waking Eve: Waking Sleeping Beauty. August 8, 2020. https://sheerahministries.com/2020/08/08/hebrew-year-5781-2021-ad-aleph-in-peysilence-in-the-mouth-part2/#:~:text=When%20we%20place%20Aleph%20in,outside%20of%20Jesus%20and%20his.

Foster, Richard J. Streams of Living Water: Celebrating the Great Traditions of Christian Faith. Grand Rapids: HarperOne, 1998.

Genius. "L.R.F. (Rollercoasters) Lyrics." Last modified 2013. https://genius.com/Jonathan-mcreynoldslrf-rollercoasters-lyrics.

Got Questions. "What Is Contemplative Prayer?." Last modified 2020. https://www.gotquestions.org/contemplative-prayer.html.

H6310 - peh - Strong's Hebrew Lexicon (KJV)." Blue Letter Bible. Accessed 28 Nov, 2020. https:www.

blueletterbible.org//lang/lexicon/lexicon cfm?Strongs=H6310&t=KJV

Hebrew for Christians. "The Letter Aleph." Last modified 2020. https://www.hebrew4christians.com/Grammar/Unit_One/Aleph-Bet/Aleph/aleph.html.

Hebrew for Christians. "The Letter Bet/Vet." Last modified 2020. https://www.hebrew4christians.com/Grammar/Unit_One/Aleph-Bet/Bet/bet.html. Hebrew for Christians. "The Letter Pey/Fey." Last modified 2020. https://www.hebrew4christians.com/Grammar/Unit_One/Aleph-Bet/Pey/pey.html.

Isaac, Tammy. Close the Door: What Happens in the Closet Stays in the Closet. Houston: T.I.M. Publishing, 2019.

Kline, Alisa. "Of Birds Lips and Baby Hawks." Buffalo Bayou (blog), n.d. https://buffalobayou.org/blog/of-bird-lips-and-baby-hawks/#:~:text=There%20are%20many%20studies%20showing,in%20the%20ultra%2Dviolet%20spectrum. &text= That%20is%20why%20as%20a,less%20likely%20to%20be%20eaten.

Marker, Craig. "Quiet Strength: What It Is and What We Can Learn from Those Who Have It." Breaking Muscle. Last modified 2020. https://breakingmuscle.com/fitness/quiet-strength-what-it-is-and-what-we-can-learn-from-those-who-have-it#:~:text=He%20or%20she%20has%20a,humility%20at%20the%20same%20time.&text=They%20are%20often%20described%20as,about%20his%20or.

Perozich, Rena. "The Year to Say What You've Seen That You Want!" The Remarkable Blog. November 8, 2019. http://rpmdaily.net/blog/the-year-to-say-what-youve-seen-that-you-want#:~:text=%E2%80%9CPey%E2%80%9D%2is%20the%20Hebrew%20letter,picture%2symbol%20of%20a%2mouth.&text=Through%20our%20mouths%20the%2breath,Breath%20of%20the%20Ho.

Placr, Simon. "Closed Mouths Don't Get Fed: The Power of Asking for What You Want." Her Campus at Murray State. May 8, 2018. https://www.hercampus.com/school/murray-state/closed-mouths-dont-get-fed-power-asking-what-you-want.

Spurgeon, Charles. "Needs to Open Our Mouths." VCY America. September 20, 2020. https://www.vcyamerica.org/charles-spurgeon/2020/09/20/needs-to-open-our-mouths/.

Texas Southern University. "About Upward Bound." Last modified 2020. http://tsu.edu/students-services/departments/trio/upward-bound/about-upward bound.html.

Trabold, Robert. "Contemplative Prayer: The Discipline of Silence." Theosophical Society. Accessed December 13, 2020. https://www.theosophical.org/publications/quest-magazine/1548-contemplative-prayer-the-discipline-of-silence.

Wikipedi The Free Encyclopedia. "Texas Cyclone." July 22, 2020. https://en.wikipedia.org/wiki/Texas_Cyclone.

Open Wide Your Mouth
TAMMY M. ISAAC, MDIV

Tammy has dedicated her life to serve God and His people. Driven by her passion to teach, mentor, and intercede for God's people in order to meet their needs. Tammy is known among her peers as a woman after God's own heart, and a woman purposed and destined to carry the gospel to those who are lost; as she increases daily in wisdom, and stature, and in favor with God and man.

With her down to earth personality she attracts young adults; allowing her to walk alongside them, helping to navigate them through life challenges with spiritual concepts. She also mentors' single adults as they trust and lean on God in they're waiting season. Sharing with them her wisdom and knowledge gained through her own personal life experiences with the guidance of the Holy Spirit.

Tammy has an anointing for intercession that is undeniable. She is a sought-after teacher/preacher of prayer, equipping intercessors and prayer teams everywhere she is called upon.

Tammy received her Bachelor of Arts in Organizational Speech Communications from Texas Southern University in December of 2011. She also received her Master of Divinity in May of 2014 from The Houston Graduate School of Theology. She then went on to study abroad at The Hebrew

University of Jerusalem in Israel during the summer of 2014. There she studied Coexistence in the Middle East and experienced the challenges of human diversity overseas where civilizations, religions and cultures converge. Tammy is currently pursuing her Doctor of Ministry degree at The Houston Graduate School of Theology.

Tammy has a heart for missions, locally and globally. She has assisted in organizing clothing drives for the Trinity Mission School (Save-A-Child) in Kenya, Africa. She also partners with low-income apartment complex to feed families during the holidays and coordinate financial resources to be given out to different ministries that need assistance. In the September of 2015 Tammy traveled to East Africa where she participated in missionary work at Maween House. Maween House is a nonprofit organization located in Kenya, East Africa. The mission of Maween House is to provide for the complete needs of orphaned and destitute children between the ages 3-7 years old.

Tammy currently resides in Houston, TX and works as a Hospice Chaplain providing spiritual and emotional support to those who have been given 6 months or less to live. Tammy volunteers at the Star of Hope Women's Shelter, participate in numerous outreach efforts in the community and is an advocate of breast cancer awareness and heart health awareness.

Made in the USA
Columbia, SC
22 April 2024